COME
DISCOVER
Christmas

COME
DISCOVER
Christmas

A 32-Day Advent Devotional

Arnold R. Fleagle

Illustrated by Timothy R. Botts

Chosen

a division of Baker Publishing Group
Minneapolis, Minnesota

Published by Chosen Books
Minneapolis, Minnesota
ChosenBooks.com

Chosen Books is a division of
Baker Publishing Group, Grand Rapids, Michigan

Printed in China

Library of Congress Cataloging-in-Publication Data
Names: Fleagle, Arnold R., author.
Title: Come discover Christmas : a 32-day advent devotional / Arnold Fleagle.
Description: Minneapolis, Minnesota : Chosen Books, a division of Baker Publishing
    Group, [2024] | Includes bibliographical references.
Identifiers: LCCN 2023058922 | ISBN 9780800763459 (cloth) | ISBN 9781493442348
    (ebook)
Subjects: LCSH: Christmas. | Devotional calendars.
Classification: LCC BV45 .F58 2024 | DDC 242/.335—dc23/eng/20240131
LC record available at https://lccn.loc.gov/2023058922

All italics in quoted Scripture passages are the emphasis of the author.

Unless otherwise indicated, Scriptures taken from the Holy Bible, New International Version®, NIV®. Copyright © 1973, 1978, 1984, 2011 by Biblica, Inc.® Used by permission of Zondervan. All rights reserved worldwide. www.zondervan.com. The "NIV" and "New International Version" are trademarks registered in the United States Patent and Trademark Office by Biblica, Inc.®

Scripture identified AMP taken from the Amplified® Bible, Copyright © 2015 by The Lockman Foundation. Used by permission. lockman.org

Cover and interior art by Timothy R. Botts
Interior design by William Overbeeke

Author represented by WordWise Media Services

Baker Publishing Group publications use paper produced from sustainable forestry practices and postconsumer waste whenever possible.

24   25   26   27   28   29   30   7   6   5   4   3   2   1

I desire to dedicate this book to my wife, Faye, and to my two sons, Matthew and Marc, for making each Christmas season so delightful and meaningful. Faye and I plan for Christmas from January through December. Our mutual love for the Savior, and her creative way of expressing that message to our family, friends, and the churches we have served, has been inspiring. Our two sons and their families have coalesced with our calendar and our faith to infuse this holy holiday with more joy and love than we ever could have anticipated!

Contents

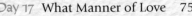

ACKNOWLEDGMENTS

I would like to especially render thanks for Chosen Books and its staff who have enthusiastically supported this project. My two editors, Kim Bangs and Natasha Sperling, have contributed their gifts, and the result is a more colorful, readable, and potentially powerful book. Also, I need to give praise to the Lord for the talents and willingness of Timothy Botts, whose calligraphy is extraordinary. Finally, my agent, David Fessenden, has believed in my vision and my writing, and his advice has been worthy of consideration and implementation.

INTRODUCTION

Come Discover Christmas is designed to serve as a road map through the colors and characters, the places and prophecies, and the sights and songs of Christmas.

You will encounter unique views on the advent of our Lord, including the ironies of Christmas, the politics of Christmas, and the inconveniences of Christmas. Several Christmas carols are unwrapped to illustrate their background and purpose. There are readings on three colors of Christmas—green, silver, and gold. My hope is that each devotion will serve to augment your understanding and celebration of this joyous season.

The coming of Jesus is a turning point in human history and eternity. This pivotal event paved the way for the Messiah to build a bridge so mankind could be reconciled to God. I pray that this volume will help clarify, and perhaps restore, the true meaning and message of Christmas.

Day 1

COME *with* ME *to* BETHLEHEM

Joseph also went up from the town of Nazareth in Galilee to Judea, to Bethlehem the town of David, because he belonged to the house and line of David.

Luke 2:4

COME WITH ME TO BETHLEHEM—a tiny town just a few miles from the major hub of Jerusalem. Though meager in demographics, its contributions to sites of biblical history are sizeable. Bethlehem was the burial site for Rachel, the beloved wife of Jacob. The greatest king of Israel, David, was born and anointed as king by Samuel in this locale. It was the prophecy of Micah, however, foretold seven centuries before Jesus' birth, that stirred the imagination and hopes among the Jewish people: "But you, Bethlehem Ephrathah, though you are small among the clans of Judah, out of you will come for me one who will be ruler over Israel, whose origins are from of old, from ancient times" (Micah 5:2). Bethlehem would cradle the *King of Kings*. It is a nonnegotiable on the Christmas tour.

How would the Lord orchestrate the fulfillment of this prophecy? He would deploy taxation through Roman emperor Caesar Augustus to guide Joseph and his expectant wife, Mary, both descendants of David, to this diminutive place of nativity. Caesar's decree nudged this couple to the exact geographic location of Micah's long-awaited fulfillment of promise. God's almighty hand utilizes methods and means, places and personnel that you and I would never contemplate to accomplish His grand plan.

The angelic choir that lit up the sky directed the shepherds to the city of David, and despite their duty to watch sheep, they raced back to Bethlehem. After the angels' departure the shepherds collectively agreed: "Let's go to Bethlehem and see this thing that has happened, which the Lord has told us about" (Luke 2:15). Their work responsibilities did not suffocate their passionate ambition to see the Savior.

But there was one group who knew where Jesus was to be born yet never searched for Him. When Herod inquired of the chief priests and scribes where the King of the Jews was to be born, they answered correctly: "In Bethlehem in Judea" (Matthew 2:5). But

neither Herod nor his advisers traveled to discover the Messiah, less than ten miles away. They were so close, so near to Bethlehem, but they never followed through on the knowledge they imparted to the seekers from far-off Medo-Persia. But the seekers, the Magi, followed the counsel of Herod's scholars and made it to Jesus.

Will you journey with me to Bethlehem this Christmas? Will you imitate the shepherds and make time and exercise effort to worship the Savior? Or will you know about Him and where to find Him, but not commit to finding a way to Bethlehem?

Jesus awaits your presence at His *birthday celebration.* Come with me to Bethlehem—you will never regret the encounter with the Son of God, the Messiah, the Christ!

Back to Bethlehem

Back to Bethlehem, let me see,
A special gift sent for me;
Heaven's priceless child from above,
Jesus Christ, the Lamb of Love.

Back to Bethlehem, let me stay,
By His manger bed where He lay;
The Holy One from high above,
Jesus Christ, the Lamb of Love.

ARNOLD R. FLEAGLE

Dear mighty God, I sometimes see myself like Bethlehem, small and seemingly insignificant. Please stretch my faith and enlarge my vision so my gifts may be significant to You, highlighting Your glory and edifying others.

Day 2

GOD BECAME *a* SINGLE CELL

Therefore the Lord himself will give you a sign: The virgin will conceive and give birth to a son, and will call him Immanuel.

Isaiah 7:14

THE IDEA OF THE CREATOR of the universe saving the world through the birth of a child catches us off guard. A human baby is the most vulnerable of all creatures. Yet the central figure of Christmas is Jesus, and His human form and frame started as a single cell. As Isaiah 7:14 details, a virgin, one who had not been intimate with a man, would conceive. Mary's conception of the Son of God was caused by none other than the Holy Spirit (Luke 1:35). The second person of the Trinity—the Son—became flesh and made His dwelling among us. The infinite became human. Jesus Christ submitted to our need for a Savior and came as one of us, lived as one of us, and died as one of us, thereby making full payment

for our failures and sins (see Romans 5:8). C. S. Lewis said it well: "The Son of God became a man to enable men to become sons of God."[1] Christmas is the great exchange!

The synergy of the eternal Spirit and Mary, a teenager from Nazareth, was a winning combination. Mary proceeded through a normal term of pregnancy, and one cell inside her became a baby boy whose very presence as a young child shuttled fear into a king. The hymnody of the season of Nativity is saturated with accolades and descriptions of the Christ child. We sing, "Glory to the newborn King," "Holy Infant so tender and mild," "Born the King of angels," and so many other carols that contain descriptions and commendations of God's Son folded into a baby's fiber and fabric. The heavenly Father can do so much with so little. Jesus stipulated that faith the size of a tiny mustard seed could move a mountain. In the manger was a tiny tot who would triumph over the world, the flesh, and the devil. And it all commenced with a single cell.

There's a Song in the Air

There's a song in the air! There's a star in the sky!
There's a mother's deep prayer and a baby's low cry!
And the star rains its fire while the beautiful sing,
For the manger of Bethlehem cradles a King![2]

Dear Father, Son, and Holy Spirit, it is incredible that Jesus was conceived by the Holy Spirit and His earthly journey began as a single cell. Likewise, our small gifts in Your holy hands can change the world. Even though I am a small drop of life in Your vast creation, use me in Your glorious Kingdom.

Day 3

SERENDIPITY

While they were there, the time came for the baby to be born, and she gave birth to her firstborn, a son. She wrapped him in cloths and placed him in a manger, because there was no guest room available for them.

Luke 2:6–7

SERENDIPITIES CAN BE DEFINED as the discovering of valuables when you weren't looking for them. These surprise treasures bring delight and prompt us to think that we have been favored. I have surprisingly found money, books, office supplies, and lost files.

For most people, the birth of Jesus caught the world unaware. Into a tiny Judean town, into a humble manger, came the Lord of the universe. C. S. Lewis remarked, "A stable once had something inside it that was bigger than our whole world."[1]

There were many prophecies that should have prepared the Jews of that time for Jesus' arrival. Isaiah had foretold that a virgin would conceive and bear a son (see Isaiah 7:14). Micah had predicted the very location of His birth, Bethlehem. In the very first book of the Old Testament, it was revealed that the Savior would come from the tribe of Judah (see Genesis 49:10). And seven hundred years prior to our Lord's birth, Jeremiah detailed that the Savior would be a descendant of King David (see Jeremiah 23:5). Despite these revelations, this prophetic child surprised many.

Perhaps the fact that Jesus had many impoverished elements associated with His nativity created a serendipitous moment. Mary and Joseph, His earthly parents, were from Nazareth, an unheralded town with a less than desirable reputation. His baby blanket was not composed of silk fibers but swaddling cloths. His crib was not elegantly carved; it was a feeding trough for cattle. The first nursery He inhabited was a stable behind an inn. And to demonstrate the low-income status of His family, Jesus' dedication offering was a pair of doves, a sacrifice to address lower-income worshipers.

Beside Jesus being a prophetic child and a poor child, the contrast of this baby possessing celebrity status caught people off guard. How many children have angels announce their conception and birth? Shepherds left their sheep, their source of livelihood, and ran to His "crib." A king was so threatened by Him that he tried to end His earthly existence at a tender age. Magi, Medo-Persian scholars, had traveled a considerable distance and brought Him expensive gifts. And this baby was assigned divine names such as

Serendipity

Immanuel, Wonderful Counselor, the Mighty God, and the Prince of Peace. His own name meant, "The Lord Saves," so every time His name was spoken, "Jesus," His mission was made public. This was one powerful child!

People found in the child Jesus a little one wrapped in prophecy, poverty, and power. The reverberations from His birth have echoed through time and throughout the world.

While Shepherds Watched Their Flocks

To you, in David's town, this day
Is born of David's line
A Savior, who is Christ the Lord,
And this shall be the sign:
The heav'nly Babe you there shall find
To human view displayed,
All meanly wrapped in swathing bands,
And in a manger laid.[2]

Dearest Lord Jesus, Your coming was a serendipity to many and Your entrance into my life a serendipity to me. I'm amazed at the difference You have made in my daily life and in the alteration of my destiny. You have lived up to Your name, "The Lord Saves," for me and so many family members and friends.

Day 4

THE CRADLE
THAT ROCKED
the WORLD

Then Simeon blessed them and said to Mary, his mother: "This child is destined to cause the falling and rising of many in Israel, and to be a sign that will be spoken against."

Luke 2:34

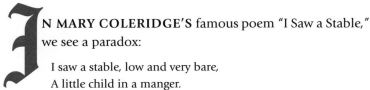

IN MARY COLERIDGE'S famous poem "I Saw a Stable," we see a paradox:

> I saw a stable, low and very bare,
> A little child in a manger.
> The oxen knew Him, had Him in their care,
> To men He was a stranger.
> The safety of the world was lying there,
> And the world's danger.[1]

For some, His cradle was the fulfillment of promise and the ray of hope; for others, it was the threat of destruction and the hollow ring of despair. The cradle of Jesus proved to be one that rocked the world.

The political world was shaken. When Herod heard the Magi's request for directions to a new king, he was visibly disturbed. His fears led him to lying and then ordering the termination of babies and small children (see Matthew 2:16–18). Jesus would further shake the political world during His apprehension and trial. The account of Pilate's wife is revealing: "While Pilate was sitting on the judge's seat, his wife sent him this message: 'Don't have anything to do with that innocent man, for I have suffered a great deal today in a dream because of him'" (Matthew 27:19). Jesus' banter with Pilate must have made his heart quiver:

> "Do you refuse to speak to me?" Pilate said. "Don't you realize I have power either to free you or to crucify you?" Jesus answered, "You would have no power over me if it were not given to you from above."
>
> John 19:10–11

The birth of the Savior sent shock waves through political hallways.

This child would alter educational norms in the first century. The Master Teacher was distinguished from some of the primary instructors of the day, "because he taught as one who had authority, and not as their teachers of the law" (Matthew 7:29). His incredible teaching was coupled with miraculous acts: "Rabbi, we know that you are a teacher who has come from God. For no one could perform the signs you are doing if God were not with him" (John 3:2). Jesus ramped up and excelled with a familiar form of storytelling, integrating thirty parables into His curriculum.

Hope

"He taught them many things by parables" (Mark 4:2). The Messiah changed the learning curve of pedagogy. Stories were easy to remember.

Jesus also agitated the "deep state" of the religious aristocracy. Take, for example, His assessment of who is granted entry into heaven. In Matthew 5:20 He elevated the prevailing standard of an acceptable lifestyle before God: "For I tell you that unless your righteousness surpasses that of the Pharisees and the teachers of the law, you will certainly not enter the kingdom of heaven." He took a hammer and chisel to the elite, proud, stiff-necked leaders of Judaism. His nicknames for their kind are very disparaging, such as "hypocrites" (Matthew 23:15), "vipers" (Matthew 12:34), and even children of the devil (see John 8:44). The Pharisees, Sadducees, and scribes displayed outward righteousness, whereas our Lord was interested in the internalization of faith, which led to a pure heart. His toppling of many practices and traditions would prompt disdain and eventually His crucifixion and death.

The birth of Jesus in Bethlehem would send shock waves through political, educational, and religious platforms. Indeed, the little one who rocked as a baby would rock the world as an adult.

Ivory Palaces

His life had also its sorrows sore,
For aloes had a part;
And when I think of the cross He bore,
My eyes with teardrops start.
Out of the ivory palaces,
Into a world of woe,
Only His great eternal love
Made my Savior go.[2]

Dear Father, Your Son changed the contour of history and eternity. I, and all those who are rescued from the kingdom of darkness and brought into the Kingdom of Light, are forever indebted to You. May I be a change agent for Jesus and look more like Him each successive day. Amen.

Day 5

A STAR *to* GUIDE

> After Jesus was born in Bethlehem in Judea, during the time of King Herod, Magi from the east came to Jerusalem and asked, "Where is the one who has been born king of the Jews? We saw his star when it rose and have come to worship him."
>
> Matthew 2:1–2

THE PHRASE "A STAR IS BORN" is not based on the movie that tracks a young and talented singer who falls in love with an established rock star. No, this phrase is about a constellation that functions as a navigational guide for the Magi as they search for the newborn baby who is the King of the Jews. They made their way to Jerusalem by following this heavenly body. There, Herod and his wise men revealed the birthplace of this royal infant: Bethlehem. "After they had heard the king, they went on their way, and the star they had seen when it rose went ahead of them until it stopped over the place where the child was" (Matthew 2:9).

What was this incredible star that lured astronomers from the East? There are several theories regarding how the Creator made and manipulated this "star." One hypothesis contends it was a conjunction of Jupiter and Saturn. Another supposition proposes it was a comet that many ancients believed heralded important political changes. A third conjecture suggests a nova, a star that has a sudden brilliant burst of light. We are not sure if any of these suppositions are valid, but the fact remains that a star guided the Magi to Jesus' home.

The star first appeared when Jesus was born, so by the time the Magi arrived in Bethlehem, our Lord's parents had moved into a house. These travelers had an enthusiastic response to the guiding star, which led them to Jesus. "When they saw the star, they were overjoyed" (Matthew 2:10). This excess joy prompted them to pursue its location and led them to worship the small Child and to lavish Him with expensive gifts: gold, frankincense, and myrrh. The gifts of the Magi were certainly very appropriate because they had just encountered the "indescribable gift," the One whose life, death, and resurrection would build a pathway of reconciliation to God. It is very possible these visitors from afar were pagans— stargazers who were intrigued by a constellation that signaled royalty had been conceived. But their responses were typical of believers who find Him even today, for they experienced great joy, humble worship, and the presentation of valuable assets—most critically the giving of oneself!

⁎
As with Gladness Men of Old

As with gladness men of old
Did the guiding star behold;
As with joy they hailed its light,
Leading onward beaming bright,
So, most gracious Lord, may we
Evermore be led to Thee.[1]

Dear Father, prevent me from losing the joy I first experienced when I embraced faith in Jesus Your Son. Assist me in maintaining a humble attitude of worship and allow me to be a faithful steward of whatever resources I have to give Him, including the sacrificial giving of myself.

Day 6

EXTRAORDINARY!

So Joseph also went up from the town of Nazareth in Galilee to Judea, to Bethlehem the town of David, because he belonged to the house and line of David.

Luke 2:4

THIS VERSE CERTAINLY could be characterized as vanilla—plain and simple. You have a poor carpenter, Joseph, from a ragtag town, Nazareth, on his way to pay taxes in Bethlehem, a locale with a population of about two thousand. The only attention-grabbing part of the verse is perhaps the mention of David, the greatest king of Israel. If you examine the Christmas narrative from this one verse only, you miss the extraordinary elements of the story that make it much more like rainbow sherbet.

Consider that the man, Joseph, is married to a woman, Mary, who has been visited by the angel Gabriel and told she is going to be the mother of the Son of God. Her partner in conceiving this elite child is not Joseph, but the Holy Spirit. Her question,

"How will this be since I am a virgin?" (Luke 1:34), did not deter the angelic messenger, because the virgin birth was God's idea, making it an astonishing event! *Extraordinary!*

We've already seen the prophecy in Micah 5:2, which predicted that little Bethlehem would be the birthplace of the Deliverer, the ruler of the nation of Israel. Why not Jerusalem? Why not Capernaum? No, Bethlehem was foretold to be the destination of this once-in-an-eternity birth! And the prophet predicted it *seven hundred years* before it happened—extraordinary!

Consider the epiphany of the angels to downcast and lowly shepherds who were scorned by the religious aristocracy. They were on night shift, watching their flocks of sheep when a single, solitary angel appeared and announced to them that a Savior had been born in David's town. This baby, wrapped in swaddling cloths and lying in a manger, was the Messiah, the Anointed One of God! If that didn't shoot up the mercury of hope in their hearts, then a whole ensemble of angels that appeared in the sky might have. They sang to them, "Glory to God in the highest." These social outcasts were the first witnesses to the birth of Jesus Christ. Now the ordinary has certainly been exchanged for the *extraordinary!*

Vanilla had been converted into rainbow sherbet. This one, humble night turned out to be the magnificent delivery hour of Jesus Christ, the King of Kings and Lord of Lords. Extraordinary!

God Rest Ye Merry, Gentlemen

God rest ye merry, gentlemen,
Let nothing you dismay,
Remember, Christ, our Saviour
Was born on Christmas day
To save us all from Satan's power
When we were gone astray.
O tidings of comfort and joy,
Comfort and joy;
O tidings of comfort and joy.[1]

Dear Father, take me to the platform of faith where I comprehend Your amazing power that transforms the ordinary into the extraordinary. I need to exercise trust that "little is much" when You are involved. The night of Jesus' birth is divine reinforcement of that truth! Amen.

THE WORD BECOMES FLESH

The Word became flesh and made his dwelling among us. We have seen his glory, the glory of the one and only Son, who came from the Father, full of grace and truth.

John 1:14

THE CHRISTMAS STORY is the incredible account of God becoming man. In theological terms this is labeled the *incarnation*. The word *incarnation* means "coming in meat" or "coming in flesh." Jesus was embodied in human skin. He was Immanuel, "God with us." C. S. Lewis, Tony Campolo, and other Christian writers have posed the question, "How could a man communicate with an ant?" The best answer: become one.

So the birth of Jesus finds the Creator becoming like the creatures He created. The world did not recognize Him (see John 1:11). His own people shunned Him. Yet He executed this transformation so that "all who did receive him, to those who believed in his name, he gave the right to become children of God" (John 1:12). The great step down, the emptying out of Himself, had a purpose: to take humans who had orphaned themselves by sin and build a bridge through His personal life and death so that they could be adopted into God's family. This exchange was accomplished through spiritual birth, not physical. Jesus had to explain this to a befuddled Jewish leader named Nicodemus. The ruler was trying to comprehend climbing back into a mother's womb when our Lord offered this explanation:

> Flesh gives birth to flesh, but the Spirit gives birth to spirit. You should not be surprised at my saying, "You must be born again." The wind blows wherever it pleases. You hear its sound, but you cannot tell where it comes from or where it is going. So it is with everyone born of the Spirit.
>
> John 3:6–8

In essence, Jesus negotiated human birth so that you and I could experience spiritual rebirth!

Paul provides a compelling account of the infinite becoming intimate with humanity in Philippians 2:6–11. In verse six he asserts that Christ Jesus was equal with God. In verse seven (AMP) he says our Lord emptied Himself and became a servant. The Greek word used is *doulos*, a bond slave. In verse eight the Messiah is described as humbling Himself and appearing as a man (*anthropos*). The extension and agony of this humility led to His obedient destination: death on a cross. The passage, however, ends with a crescendo, for in verses nine through eleven, Jesus is exalted, His name is above every name, and every knee bows to Him in heaven

The
Word
becomes
flesh

and on earth. Tongues that wagged at Him will join tongues that praised Him and confess that *He is Lord!*

The story of a little girl who climbed up and sat on her mother's knee says it all. She looked up at her mother and made this request: "Mommy, tell me a story of Jesus and put me in it." Through the incarnation, Jesus became one of us so that we could become a son or daughter of God the Father!

The Incarnation

The great God of Heaven is come down to earth,
His Mother a Virgin, and sinless His Birth;
The Father eternal His Father alone:
He sleeps in the manger; He reigns on the Throne.

Then let us adore Him,
And praise His great love,
To save us poor sinners
He came from above.[1]

Dear heavenly Father, the incarnation of Jesus both inspires me and humbles me. Your plan for His coming, and His willingness to become one of His created beings, is indescribable and unthinkable love. Remind me of this love when I doubt Your affection for me! I confess my ungrateful attitude and actions that betray such transcendent devotion and sacrifice.

Day 8

PROPHECY
FULFILLED

He said to them, "This is what I told you while I was still with you:
Everything must be fulfilled that is written about me in the Law of
Moses, the Prophets and the Psalms."

Luke 24:44

E NOW HAVE "Christmas in July." This prema-
ture marketing annoys those of us who want to
enjoy summer and fall before we dive into the
ambitious Christmas calendar. But the biggest
"offenders" of promoting Christmas early are no longer around—
the prophets who advanced the birth of Jesus centuries before it
became history. Isaiah trimmed his Christmas tree seven hundred
years before Jesus was born.

One of the most phenomenal predictions in the book of Isaiah
is centered around the virgin birth of Jesus. "Therefore the Lord
himself will give you a sign: The virgin will conceive and give

birth to a son, and will call him Immanuel" (Isaiah 7:14). This is one of the most quoted verses in apologetics for the veracity of God's Word. It came true: A teenage virgin, Mary of Nazareth, who had never been intimate with a man, gave birth to the Son of God. The Holy Spirit came over this young maiden and by His power blessed her womb (see Luke 1:35). One of the Son's handles would be "Immanuel," which means "God with us"! Not only did Isaiah forecast that a Messianic figure would be born, but the revered prophet indicated the immense importance of His role.

> For to us a child is born, to us a son is given, and the government will be on his shoulders. And he will be called Wonderful Counselor, Mighty God, Everlasting Father, Prince of Peace. Of the greatness of his government and peace there will be no end. He will reign on David's throne and over his kingdom, establishing and upholding it with justice and righteousness from that time on and forever. The zeal of the LORD Almighty will accomplish this.
>
> Isaiah 9:6–7

Imagine the potency of the statement that "the government will be on his shoulders." This child would reign on David's exalted throne and maintain justice and righteousness, which is evident with the youth's impressive names: Wonderful Counselor, Mighty God, the Everlasting Father, and the Prince of Peace.

A third prophecy spoke to the genealogy of Jesus: "A shoot will come up from the stump of Jesse; from his roots a Branch will bear fruit" (Isaiah 11:1). Jesse was the father of David. The line of the Deliverer's descent was predetermined. Bethlehem was the birthplace of David and it was also the birthplace of Jesus. The small town of about two thousand residents cradled the King of Kings.

I heard that a general superintendent of a denomination once made this remark: "If my foresight was like my hindsight, I'd be out-of-sight." God's Word has been unquestionably proven to possess this kind of foresight! This heightens our hope and adds to our confidence that God has command of history and eternity.

Of the Father's Love Begotten

This is He whom seers in old time
Chanted of with one accord,
Whom the voices of the prophets
Promised in their faithful word.
Now He shines, the long-expected;
Let creation praise its Lord
Evermore and evermore.[1]

Dear long-expected Jesus, Your first coming found many flat-footed, unprepared. I invite You to keep me alert and anticipating Your glorious second coming. I do not want to be caught off guard. I am so confident that You remember Your prophecies and that all the predictions find their yes in You.

Day 9

THE IRONIES
of CHRISTMAS

The Word became flesh and made his dwelling among us. We have seen his glory, the glory of the one and only Son, who came from the Father, full of grace and truth.

John 1:14

*I*RONY IS "the use of words to express something other than and especially the opposite of the literal meaning."[1] Consider the irony of time. History is often viewed as an endless cycle repeated over and over without direction, whereas the Christian view of history is the opposite—it is linear, having a beginning and an end. Romans 8:28 tells us that "all things work together for good." History is not happenstance. Ephesians 1:11 declares that God "works out everything in conformity with the purpose of his will," which means there is a master plan! Jeremiah 29:11 pertains to the individual and asserts: "For I know the plans I have for you . . . plans to prosper you and not

to harm you, plans to give you hope and a future." The beautiful
irony is that the eternal God has invaded time and space to use
finite beings to accomplish everlasting purposes. To secular man,
this is totally unexpected.

Consider the irony of power. Christians believe in an Almighty
God who wrapped Himself in human skin and whose "weakness"
in this mode is stronger than our greatest enemy, death. The in-
carnate Christ came as a baby, the most helpless of all creatures.
The Lord Jesus needed His diapers changed. The King of Kings
was born to poor parents, was raised in a town with an atrocious
reputation, and was subject to the care of those He had created.
Jesus stooped low that we might attain heavenly places. The prince
became a pauper, and the pauper became a prince (see Isaiah 9:6)!

Consider the irony of love. Man seldom knows whom to love, or how to love, or whom he loves best. Jesus' love is so purposeful and sacrificial that He allowed Himself to be destroyed to save others. John 3:16 reminds us "For God so loved the world that he gave . . ." And "God demonstrates his own love for us in this: While we were still sinners, Christ died for us" (Romans 5:8). First John 4:10 highlights the irony in these terms: "This is love: not that we loved God, but that he loved us and sent his Son as an atoning sacrifice for our sins." God's love motivated Christ's death. The shepherd typically raises sheep that are then sold for a profit; in this case the God-Child of Christmas spends His life for the profit of His flock. In the Chronicles of Narnia, the powerful lion king, Aslan, allows himself to be slain for a traitor. Such is the irony of divine love!

So the Christmas story has folded into it the ironies of time, power, and love. The more we develop a relationship with the Lord, the more we study His personality in His Word, and the more we reflect on the good gifts He invests in our lives, the more these incredible ironies seem *normal* and *expected* for Him.

There's a Song in the Air

There's a song in the air! There's a star in the sky!
There's a mother's deep prayer and a baby's low cry!
And the star rains its fire while the beautiful sing,
For the manger of Bethlehem cradles a King![2]

Thank You, Father, for the unexpected ironies of Christmas. I am indebted to Your gracious plan of salvation through which You dealt decisively with my sins through the birth, life, death, and resurrection of Jesus. Your grace erased my disgrace, and I am now a privileged member of Your family.

Day 10

THE POLITICS
of CHRISTMAS

When Herod realized that he had been outwitted by the Magi, he
was furious, and he gave orders to kill all the boys in Bethlehem
and its vicinity who were two years old and under, in accordance
with the time he had learned from the Magi.

Matthew 2:16

CHRISTMAS IS POLITICAL because a new King is
born who would establish a new world order. The
birth of Jesus began an insurrection against the powers and potentates on the earth. Caesar would issue
a taxation decree that would bring Jesus' family to Bethlehem,
where the prophet Micah predicted He would be born. King Herod
would be threatened and execute a wholesale assassination of
all male babies under the age of two in and around Bethlehem.
Later, the governor, Pontius Pilate, would sanction the death of

A new
King
is born

Jesus after the religious leaders accuse Him of opposing Caesar (see John 19:12, 15–16).

Jeremiah 23:5 highlighted the promise of a King coming from David's royal line:

> "The days are coming," declares the LORD, "when I will raise up for David a righteous Branch, a King who will reign wisely and do what is just and right in the land."

David was the greatest king of Israel. His reign had been the high point of Israel's history. This wise and future King would be produced through David's DNA. This connection would make this baby dangerous to Israel's enemies.

The senior citizen Simeon predicted that this baby would be a political leader who was "destined to cause the falling and rising of many in Israel" (Luke 2:34). Jesus Christ would throw Israel into a free fall. Some would be drawn to faith through Him, others would stumble over Him. Herod, appointed by the Roman Empire to rule over Jews, would be intimidated by the news brought by the Magi. Not only Herod was disturbed, but *all Jerusalem* (see Matthew 2:3). The birth of Jesus meant that an old order of life was over—similar to our lives when the King enters and transforms our nature and changes our destiny. God is interested in the affairs of men and is not detached from them. This intervention affects the political, moral, and spiritual affairs of mankind.

Angels from the Realms of Glory

Angels, from the realms of glory,
Wing your flight o'er all the earth;
Ye who sang creation's story,
Now proclaim Messiah's birth:
Come and worship,
Come and worship,
Worship Christ, the newborn King.[1]

Dear ruler of my heart, You have come in and overcome the sinful regime that had controlled me. Thank You that I am a new creature with a new future because the old order has been toppled by love and grace.

MARVELOUS
MYSTERY

For God was pleased to have all his fullness dwell in him.

Colossians 1:19

THE MYSTERY OF THE AGES that filters into the Christmas narrative is this: *Jesus is fully God and fully man.* In theological terms this is described as "the hypostatic union," Christ's human and divine natures coexisting in one person. The epic Church Council of Chalcedon (AD 451) framed this union in these terms:

> Christ . . . to be acknowledged in *two natures, inconfusedly, unchangeably, indivisibly, inseparably* . . . concurring in *one Person* . . . not parted or divided into two persons, but one and the same Son, and only begotten, God, the Word, the Lord Jesus Christ (emphasis added).[1]

The existence of these two natures is supported by Scripture. Christ's divine nature has a truckload of evidence. Jesus demonstrated His omnipotence when He calmed the storm at sea with one word (see Matthew 8:26–27). His omniscience is present when He knew people's thoughts (see Matthew 12:25) and knew Nathanael before He ever saw him (see John 1:48). When Jesus turned water into wine, He manifested the glory of God (see John 2:11). He contended for His eternal existence by declaring, "Before Abraham was born, I am" (John 8:58). He did not argue with His critics when they questioned His identity, but after forgiving the paralytic's sin, He proceeded to heal him (see Mark 2:5–12).

The proof for Christ's human nature is not deficient either. He was born a baby like you and me (see Luke 2:7). He became fatigued like you and me (see John 4:6). He grew hungry like you and me (see Matthew 4:2). Our Lord thirsted when He lacked water (see John 4:7). And God's Son bled just like you and me when His body was pierced (see John 19:34).

Jesus lived the most extraordinary life ever witnessed in the history of this planet. Just compare Him to Caesar Augustus, the

Roman emperor who sat on the throne when Jesus was born. Caesar Augustus taxed the whole world to receive payment; Jesus came to make payment for the whole world. Caesar Augustus won his kingdom at the battle of Actium; Jesus Christ won His Kingdom at the cross of Calvary. Caesar Augustus would reign for decades; Jesus would reign forever and ever. Caesar Augustus exalted himself in order to perpetuate his legacy among men; Jesus Christ humbled Himself to extend the legacy and lives of men. This God-Man has no equal!

The People That in Darkness Sat

For unto us a Child of hope is born,
To us a Son is giv'n,
And on His shoulders ever rests
All pow'r in earth and heav'n.[2]

Dear Lord Jesus, I am amazed at Your willingness to surrender Your place beside the Father to take my place on the cross. You truly are beyond description and definition. May I share with others Your deity and humanity wrapped up as one "indescribable gift" (2 Corinthians 9:15).

BREAD *of* LIFE

But you, Bethlehem Ephrathah, though you are small among the clans of Judah, out of you will come for me one who will be ruler over Israel, whose origins are from of old, from ancient times.

Micah 5:2

 LITTLE TOWN OF BETHLEHEM" was written by one of America's foremost preachers, Phillip Brooks (1835–1893). Years earlier, he had visited the Holy Land and spent time in Bethlehem on Christmas Eve. Then, when Brooks was searching for a new Christmas carol for the children of his church to sing, he pulled from his time in Bethlehem and wrote the words. Lewis Redner, his Sunday school superintendent and organist, could not come up with the right tune for the song until he woke from his sleep the night before the program hearing music, which he composed as the tune to go along with the lyrics. Redner insisted the tune was a gift from heaven.[1]

BREAD OF LIFE

Bethlehem is a significant biblical town by virtue of many important people who were associated with it. Just a few miles south of Jerusalem, it is the burial ground for Rachel, Jacob's wife. More substantially, it is the birthplace of David, the premiere king of Israel. David was a shepherd in the fields surrounding Bethlehem, as were the shepherds who were directed to Bethlehem to witness the newborn Savior. The name Bethlehem fittingly means "House of Bread," as it was the birthplace of "the Bread of Life" (John 6:35 AMP).

At a population of two thousand, we might be tempted to dismiss Bethlehem as tiny, but God often utilizes minor elements to accomplish His purposes. The Israelites were the fewest of all peoples (see Deuteronomy 7:7). David was the youngest of Jesse's sons (see 1 Samuel 16:11). Elijah's rain cloud was as small as a man's hand (see 1 Kings 18:44). Faith, the size of a minuscule mustard seed, can move mountains (see Matthew 17:20). A boy's lunch fed a multitude (see John 6:9–13). The tongue is not a sizeable component of our bodies, but it has the potential to do devastating damage (see James 3:5). Bethlehem fits into this principle: little can be big if it is in the tool chest of the Father.

Bethlehem is a prophetic city. Micah predicted Bethlehem as the birthplace of Israel's ruler (see Micah 5:2). Bethlehem was foretold as a city of great sorrow (see Jeremiah 31:15). The prophecy came true, and Bethlehem was the site of a terrible massacre (see Matthew 2:16–18). Hosea predicted a son would be called out of Egypt (see 11:1). This was fulfilled when Bethlehem said goodbye to the child Jesus, whose parents escaped to Egypt to avoid King Herod's wrath (see Matthew 2:13).

Bethlehem is a reminder not to discount the metrics that are not impressive because little is much when God is in it. Bruce Barton made this perceptive observation: "Sometimes when I consider what tremendous consequences come from little things, I am tempted to think there are no little things."[2] The little town of Bethlehem became a big player in the Christmas narrative.

O Little Town of Bethlehem

O little town of Bethlehem, how still we see thee lie!
Above thy deep and dreamless sleep the silent stars go by.
Yet in thy dark streets shineth, the everlasting light;
The hopes and fears of all the years are met in thee tonight.[3]

Dear Lord Almighty, forgive me for using metrics to decide what can be a tool in Your hands. Too often I use appearances to decide what instruments work best to achieve Your plans. You have a much more discerning view that looks at availability more than ability, and humility rather than prestige and pride. Remind me that You can do whatever You want, with whomever You want, wherever You want, and however You want in fulfilling Your will!

PEACE *on* EARTH

Glory to God in the highest heaven, and on earth peace to those on whom his favor rests.

Luke 2:14

THE POEM "CHRISTMAS BELLS," which later became the basis for the carol "I Heard the Bells on Christmas Day," was written by the highly regarded writer Henry Wadsworth Longfellow. The bells of sorrow had rung for him when he lost two family members. His wife tragically died in 1861 from burns sustained after her dress caught fire. Then Longfellow's oldest son, Lieutenant Charles Appleton Longfellow, was severely wounded in the Civil War. The poem was written just six months after the Battle of Gettysburg, where there were more than forty thousand casualties. While hearing the ringing of Christmas bells, he was inspired to write this poem. Longfellow had faith God would overcome this terrible war and bring peace.[1] He ends the poem with words based on the refrain of the angels in Luke 2, "On earth peace to those on whom his

PEACE ON EARTH

favor rests" (verse 14). Like the prophets Isaiah and Jeremiah, Longfellow found a silver lining in the storm clouds of destruction and war.

Throughout history there have been bells of "man's inhumanity to man." The first family witnessed Cain killing his brother Abel. The Jewish people suffered under five consecutive empires that exacted blood, money, and property from them. Our Easter celebration features man's inhumanity to the God-Man, Jesus Christ.

Jeremiah's indictment is blunt: "Peace, peace . . . when there is no peace" (6:14). Longfellow would echo the weeping prophet's sentiments in stanza 6: "And in despair I bowed my head; 'There is no peace on earth,' I said." World War I (1914–1918) was nicknamed "The War to End All Wars." Yet we have had many wars since, and here we are in the twenty-first century with threats on many fronts. Our frustration parallels Longfellow's as we search for peace but have found it chronically elusive.

We do possess bells of hope and peace. Isaiah, called the Evangelist of the Old Covenant, predicted a "Prince of Peace" seven hundred years before the birth of Jesus. The nation of Israel was about to be run over by the Assyrian horde, but he planted a noble thought in their minds: peace! The New Testament includes the word *peace* in twenty-six of its twenty-seven books.

The primary term for peace in the New Testament is *eirene*, which is used to translate the Hebrew word *shalom*. Ephesians 2:14 declares, "For he himself is our peace, who has made the two groups one and has destroyed the barrier, the dividing wall of hostility" (between Jews and Gentiles). A well-known bumper sticker reads: "Know Jesus, Know Peace. No Jesus, No Peace." There is a manger in every man's heart and Jesus desires to occupy it and bring genuine peace to our existence.

In 1962, Don and Carol Richardson went as missionaries to the Sawi people of Irian Jaya, the western part of New Guinea, to a society based upon deceit and treachery. Working with three different tribes, Don and Carol encountered constant fighting, and many times lives were lost. Finally, a man named Kaiyo offered his only son to a man named Mahor of a competing tribe. In return, Mahor offered his son to Kaiyo. The exchange of the two babies ended the war and brought peace to the Sawis.[2] Each child was considered "a peace child." The Richardsons used this illustration to teach about the Prince of Peace, a Son offered by the heavenly Father to cease the wars of sin that raged in human hearts.

I Heard the Bells on Christmas Day

Then pealed the bells more loud and deep,
"God is not dead, nor does He sleep;
The wrong shall fail, the right prevail,
With peace on earth, good will to men."

Till ringing, singing on its way,
The world revolved from night to day,
A voice, a chime, a chant sublime
Of peace on earth, good will to men.[3]

Dear Father, I have sought for peace through many methods and in many places. May my default search be to look to Jesus, the Author and Completer of my peace.

Day 14

HOLY NIGHT

And there were shepherds living out in the fields nearby, keeping watch over their flocks at night.

Luke 2:8

"SILENT NIGHT" was the product of two men, Father Joseph Mohr, a Roman Catholic priest, and his organist, Franz Gruber. They had set out to write "the perfect Christmas hymn," but when the organ broke on Christmas Eve, Mohr decided he would not disappoint his congregation and wrote just the lyrics. Gruber, when he saw the words for this revered Christmas carol, remarked, "You have found it—the right song—God be praised."[1]

Stanza 1 is about a virgin birth. Mary, estimated to be fourteen to sixteen years of age, was engaged to Joseph, a poor carpenter. Both were descendants of King David. The angel Gabriel was sent to deliver this message: "Greetings, you who are highly favored! The Lord is with you" (Luke 1:28). This troubled Mary, but the angel went on to say,

> You will conceive and give birth to a son, and you are to call him Jesus. He will be great and will be called the Son of the Most High. The Lord God will give him the throne of his father David.

Luke 1:31–32

Mary consented to be the Lord's servant and bore the Savior of the world. "Silent Night" acknowledges this reality:

> Silent night, holy night,
> All is calm, all is bright
> Round yon virgin, mother and child;
> Holy infant, so tender and mild,
> Sleep in heavenly peace,
> Sleep in heavenly peace.

Stanza 2 focuses on the quaking shepherds. When the angel appeared to inform them of Jesus' birth, these men were shaken to their core (see Luke 2:9). There are many famous shepherds in the Old Testament, such as Moses and David. By the time of the New Testament, however, this profession had lost its cachet. Even though they were keeping sheep for the temple sacrifices, they could not attend temple worship services themselves and were considered outcasts. Though religious leaders had stigmatized them and looked down on them, God the Father made them the first witnesses to the birth of His Son. After seeing the Messiah with their own eyes, they ran from the birth site and became the first evangelists of the Savior's arrival to this world: "The shepherds returned, glorifying and praising God for all the things they had heard and seen, which were just as they had been told" (Luke 2:20).

> Silent night, holy night,
> Shepherds quake at the sight;
> Glories stream from heaven afar,
> Heavenly hosts sing, "Alleluia!
> Christ the Savior is born!
> Christ the Savior is born!"

The third stanza focuses on the beauty and identity of the baby. This was God's holy Son and He radiated beauty to the world. The Father had intervened to save men from their transgressions and replaced their failures with redeeming grace. Many churches who sing this carol at the climax of the candle-lighting service

raise their candles to spread the light through their sanctuary or worship center during the singing of the third stanza.

> Silent night, holy night,
> Son of God, love's pure light
> Radiant beams from Thy holy face
> With the dawn of redeeming grace,
> Jesus, Lord, at Thy birth!
> Jesus, Lord, at Thy birth![2]

Dear Father of our Lord Jesus Christ, I render praise and thanksgiving that earth is the visited planet. You made our problem Your problem and resolved it through Jesus. May my life spread the message of His light to an ever-darkening world.

Day 15

ANGELS SING

Suddenly a great company of the heavenly host appeared with the angel, praising God and saying, "Glory to God in the highest heaven, and on earth peace to those on whom his favor rests."

Luke 2:13–14

THE GREEK WORD FOR ANGEL is *angelos*, which means "messenger." The Hebrew word is *mal'ak*, "one who is sent with a message." The word *angel* and its plural appear 386 times in the English Bible. How many angels are there? Revelation 5:11–13 answers the question: "thousands upon thousands, and ten thousand times ten thousand." An angel is a supernatural being, greater and more powerful than man, who carries messages from God to certain individuals and groups, sometimes bringing judgment. Angels also guard, fight, and protect human beings. The word *angel* is always in masculine form.[1]

Angels are woven throughout the Christmas story; they appear eighteen different times! Joseph has several visits from angels.

In Matthew 1, an angel appears to him in a dream and instructs him to take Mary as his wife and to give the boy child the name Jesus (verses 20–21). In a later dream, Joseph is told by an angel to escape to Egypt because Herod is planning to murder Jesus (Matthew 2:13). After Herod died, an angel appeared to Joseph again and directed him to return to Israel because Herod and those seeking Jesus' life were dead (Matthew 2:19–20).

Zechariah the priest was in the sanctuary when he encountered Gabriel, an angel, who disclosed to him that his aged wife, Elizabeth, was going to bear a child and this boy's name was to be John. Because the priest demonstrated unbelief, he could not speak until the child was born (Luke 1:18–22).

Gabriel's appearance to Mary is frequently referenced in the telling of the greatest story ever told. It is well-known that the angel revealed Mary as God's choice to be the mother of Jesus. Even though she was a virgin—had never known a man intimately—a baby would grow in her womb, and this child would be the Son of God (Luke 1:35).

The shepherds on the Judean hillside near Bethlehem experienced an angelic epiphany that terrified them (Luke 2:9). They were informed that fear was not necessary for good news came with him, namely, that the Savior of the world was born that day (see Luke 2:11). After giving a description of the baby's dress and resting place, a host of angels praised God with "Glory to God" and "Peace on earth" (Luke 2:13–14).

"Hark! the Herald Angels Sing" was written by Charles Wesley, brother of the English revival speaker John Wesley. The tune was composed by Felix Mendelssohn, a famous German pianist. Charles was a prolific hymn writer and penned over 6,500 hymns. "Hark! the Herald Angels Sing" has been designated by many as the most popular of all Christmas hymns. Stanza 1's theme highlights the King who has come to reconcile sinners to God. Stanza 2's hallmark presents Christ as God in the flesh, the incarnation. Stanza 3 declares that this meek and mild baby will conquer death by giving humans a second birth. The final stanza is an invitation that extends to all nations, to allow this Christ to live and work in our lives and *reconnect us to God's everlasting and incomparable love.*

Hark! the Herald Angels Sing

Hark! the herald angels sing,
"Glory to the newborn King!
Peace on earth and mercy mild;
God and sinners reconciled."
Joyful, all ye nations rise,
Join the triumph of the skies;
With angelic hosts proclaim,
"Christ is born in Bethlehem."
Hark! the herald angels sing,
"Glory to the newborn King!"[2]

Dear heavenly Father, You have revealed Yourself in diverse ways. The angels, who do Your bidding, made a dramatic impact in the Christmas story. I am especially thankful for their message of a Savior. I am so amazed at how many ways You accomplish Your purposes and how many instruments You employ in achieving Your perfect will!

Day 16

PROMISES KEPT

Sovereign Lord, as you have promised, you may now dismiss your servant in peace. For my eyes have seen your salvation, which you have prepared in the sight of all nations: a light for revelation to the Gentiles, and the glory of your people Israel.

Luke 2:29–32

SIMEON WAS A MAN who had lived most of his life by the time of Jesus' birth—he was in his eleventh hour on earth. The Holy Spirit had made a promise to this saintly senior that "he would not die before he had seen the Lord's Messiah" (Luke 2:26). Jewish law stipulated that firstborn sons were to be redeemed (see Exodus 13:12–13), and that after the birth of a son, the mother was to go through the right of purification after forty days (see Leviticus 12:1–4). This redemption and ending of purification took place at the same time, and it set the stage for Simeon's encounter with the baby Jesus.

Moved by the Spirit, Simeon, a righteous and devout man, made his way to the temple. By divine timing, Mary and Joseph also traveled the few miles from Bethlehem to Jerusalem to bring baby Jesus to the temple, "to do for him what the custom of the Law required" (Luke 2:27). This intersection of Simeon and Jesus' family led to a song that has been titled "The Nunc Dimittis," from the initial words of the Latin Vulgate translation, meaning "you may now dismiss."

Simeon's song, our Scripture reading above, is a praise song that confirms the Lord had remembered His promise: Simeon's eyes had seen God's salvation. Now death would be experienced peacefully, since the Holy Spirit's promise to him had been fulfilled. Simeon acknowledged the impact of this Messiah would cover both Jews and Gentiles. Subsequent to his song, Simeon

blessed Joseph and Mary and made the first mention in the New Testament of Jesus' suffering and death, as well as the hurt Mary would experience in the future: "And a sword will pierce your own soul too" (Luke 2:35).

Another senior citizen, Anna, a prophetess who visited the temple night and day, came up during Simeon's rendezvous with the Savior and rendered thanksgiving for the baby. She forecast a favorable future: "She gave thanks to God and spoke about the child to all who were looking forward to the redemption of Jerusalem" (Luke 2:38).

God the Father had a prominent place for seniors in the birth narratives of Jesus. An article in the *Los Angeles Times* quoted Dilip Jeste, a geriatric psychiatrist: "The stigma [against elders] is growing." Another source quoted in the article said, "It's open season for discrimination against older, vulnerable people."[1] The Lord does not hold to this opinion. His Word shows the elderly in roles of leadership and respect. Simeon and Anna were faithful to God and His casting of them in the "Greatest Story Ever Told" is noteworthy. If you are a senior, make yourself available for being an instrument in His hands. If you are younger, don't discount the gifts and experience of the aging! Consider the admonition of Leviticus 19:32: "Stand up in the presence of the aged, show respect for the elderly and revere your God. I am the LORD."

What Child Is This?

Why lies He in such mean estate
Where ox and donkeys are feeding?
Good Christians, fear, for sinners here
The silent Word is pleading
Nails, spears shall pierce Him through
the cross He bore for me, for you
Hail, hail the Word made flesh
the Babe, the Son of Mary.[2]

Dear Lord of All, please assist me in recognizing Your gifts in all shapes and sizes, all ages and colors, and all different strata of the economic spectrum. You enlist the breadth and depth of humanity in Your great plan of salvation. I am so thankful that You franchised me into Your family, and You have deployed me in your sacred work.

WHAT MANNER
of LOVE

For God so loved the world that he gave his one and only Son, that
whoever believes in him shall not perish but have eternal life. For
God did not send his Son into the world to condemn the world,
but to save the world through him.

John 3:16–17

THE VERSES ABOVE comprise what many Bible
students and scholars call "the miniature gospel."
The thrust of John 3:16 is a loving God who has dealt
decisively with the problem of mankind's sin by sac-
rificing His Son, Jesus, to heal our souls from the cancer that was
destroying them. Dorothy Sayers summed up the Father's solution
in these terms: "God chose to make man as he is—limited and
suffering and subject to sorrows and death—He had the honesty
and the courage to take His own medicine."[1] One way to define
love is "making your problem my problem." Paul described the

what manner of LOVE

process with this Spirit-led observation: "God made him who had no sin to be sin for us, so that in him we might become the righteousness of God" (2 Corinthians 5:21).

The Greeks had three words for love. *Eros* does not appear in the Greek New Testament. It refers to *glandular* love. Animals operate on this level and do not discriminate with their partners for they are only concerned with glandular satisfaction. The word *erotic* comes from this word. The second word for love is *phileo*. Although it is sometimes substituted for the highest level of love, it often is employed for *reciprocal* or *quid pro quo* love: "You scratch my back and I'll scratch yours." The third and final word for love is *agape*. This love is *unconditional*. It is not dependent upon the one who receives love. The wedding vows spoken by a bride and groom, "for better or for worse, for richer or for poorer, for sickness or for health," frames love with no conditions. This is the love of God. Romans 5:8 gives a sample of His agape love: "But

God demonstrates his own love for us in this: While we were still sinners, Christ died for us."

What did the Lord see in us? Did He need more possessions? No, He already owned everything (see Psalm 50:9–12). Did we appear as an attractive catch? No, Isaiah 64:6 catalogues the merchandise: "All of us have become like one who is unclean, and all our righteous acts are like filthy rags; we all shrivel up like a leaf, and like the wind our sins sweep us away."

The greater question is this: What do we see in the heavenly Father and His Son? At Christmas, Jesus became one of us so we might become the sons and daughters of God (see John 1:9–14). We observe a Savior who loved us first and did not wait for us to make the first move toward Him (see 1 John 4:19). And this Jesus emptied Himself and became obedient to the point of death, even the barbaric torture of the cross (see Philippians 2:6–8). Love was redefined when God came down at Christmas in the person of His beloved Son!

The classic story is told of the little boy who made himself a boat. He took it down to the ocean and, unfortunately, the tide took his boat out to sea. One day he was riding his bike in town and saw his boat in a store window. He proceeded to go inside and talk to the owner and inform him that he would like to take his boat home. He was told that the boat would cost $3.00. Going home to his father and describing his dilemma, his dad agreed to give him chores until he had earned the purchase price. Finally earning the required fee, he marched into the store, found the owner, and handed him the money with these words: "I made it, I lost it, I bought it back." This parallels the Lord, for *He made us*, *He lost us*, and *He bought us back*.

Love Came Down at Christmas

Love came down at Christmas,
Love all lovely, Love divine;
Love was born at Christmas;
Star and angels gave the sign.[2]

Dear heavenly Father, You displayed unconditional, agape love in the Christmas story. I was dirty and dead in my sins when You gifted Jesus to reverse and renovate me. I am so indebted to You for bringing me back into Your family.

Day 18

JOY *in the* FORECAST

Fixing our eyes on Jesus, the pioneer and perfecter of faith. For the joy set before him he endured the cross, scorning its shame, and sat down at the right hand of the throne of God.

Hebrews 12:2

CHRISTMAS MINISTRY in a local church exacts a high payment from its people. Additional planning, unexpected time investments, surprise challenges from weather, necessary rehearsal cancellations—all of this assaults our calendar. This season of faith and fulfillment can spawn feelings of frustration and impose a collar of inconvenience on our lifestyles. The first Christmas also shuttled inconvenience in epic proportions for those God chose to participate in the greatest story ever told.

A teenager and her husband found their lives rocked by an angel's prophecy that they would be the earthly parents of the Son of God. Inconvenience was endemic to this impoverished couple

JOY IN THE FORECAST

who resided in the disreputable town of Nazareth. They would be the target of misguided critics. They would bear the labels "irreligious" and "immoral." The baby would rest inside Mary's womb during a seventy-six-mile journey over less-than-ideal terrain. A "No Vacancy" sign would await them when they sought shelter at an inn. The glorious birth would, in the near future, mandate a quick getaway to Egypt. But their desire to be obedient to God's call as earthly parents of God's Son would outweigh the cost of inconvenience.

The shepherds were startled during the night watch when the heavenly agents announced the birth of Jesus and served as a GPS to His location. Inconvenience was evident since their schedules did not include a visit to the manger, which would leave their flocks vulnerable on the hillsides. Nevertheless, the ecstasy of eternity invading time in the form of a new baby boy outweighed the risk of forsaking their flocks and sprinting to David's city.

This incredible birth had its own heavenly prop—a natal star. The constellation appeared and lit the imagination of the wise men, who left their comfortable milieu to seek a deity of another race and faith. Miles were traveled, life and limb were placed in jeopardy before a jealous King Herod, and precious gifts were surrendered to a baby. The desire to see the King of the Jews outweighed the cost and inconvenience at this first Christmas.

Christmas means a Son, the firstborn of heaven, was away from home. From splendor to squalor, from invincible to vulnerable, from angels to fallen humanity, down the staircase of heaven to a cattle-feeding trough, indeed, our Lord was inconvenienced! It's illogical, it's inconceivable, but this is the lovely Jesus. The richest of all became poor, confined to time and space, and endured attacks and eventually death. All for the joy that was set before Him: the redemption of the human race.

Gentle Mary
Laid Her Child

Gentle Mary laid her Child
Lowly in a manger;
He is still the undefiled,
But no more a stranger:
Son of God, of humble birth,
Beautiful the story;
Praise His Name in all the earth,
Hail the King of glory![1]

Dear Father, Son, and Holy Spirit, the cost of Christmas was extraordinary for heaven and for the characters who played a part on earth. Forgive me for my impatience, my unwillingness to sacrifice, my shallow understanding of the greater good as You achieve Your plan, at times, through inconvenience. Make me more like Mary, Joseph, the shepherds, and the wise men in this regard. Amen.

Day 19

THE FLASH
of CHRISTMAS:
GOOD NEWS!

But the angel said to them, "Do not be afraid. I bring you good news that will cause great joy for all the people."

Luke 2:10

N MY MINISTRY CAREER I have often been chosen to deliver difficult news. Some glimpses into this occupational hazard include breaking the news to parents that their child has been born with Down syndrome, or sharing with family members that a loved one is dying or has taken his final breath. But I was also the voice declaring someone had been saved, or that a patient had just received a positive prognosis after a life-threatening illness. To illustrate the "good news, bad news" yo-yo, I was in my office one day and within thirty minutes I was informed one baby was born and another baby had died. Needless to say, it

GOOD NEWS

is much more gratifying to share the good news and be welcomed because you bring sunlight into a tense room.

Angels are often God's mailmen. Sometimes they deliver messages of doom and gloom. In the Old and New Testaments, however, there are many examples of them carrying messages that result in positive outcomes. Angels directed Lot to flee from Sodom, which saved his life (see Genesis 19:15). An angel stopped Abraham from taking Issac's life, sparing the generational line of the future Savior (see Genesis 22:11–12). These rescue operations continue in the New Testament, such as the angel's role in liberating Peter from prison just prior to his looming death (see Acts 12:7). Angels also acted as EMTs to provide healing resources to Elijah (see 1 Kings 19:5), and even to Jesus after His temptation via Satan (see Matthew 4:11).

Another assignment for these agents of heaven is to be guardians and protectors of God's family. David highlighted this ministry in Psalm 34:7, "The angel of the LORD encamps around those who fear him, and he delivers them." Daniel testified to this service when he reported that God sent an angel that shut the lions' mouths after he had spent the night in their den (see Daniel 6:22). And Jesus said this about children: "Their angels in heaven always see the face of my Father" (Matthew 18:10).

In the Christmas narrative, angels are recurrently sharing good news. An angel reported to Zechariah that his aged wife, Elizabeth, would give birth to John the Baptist (see Luke 1:13). Mary was informed by Gabriel she would be the mother of God's Son (see Luke 1:35). It was an angel who told Joseph to marry the virgin Mary because she was with child of the Holy Spirit (see Matthew 1:20). The great joy announcement to the shepherds was transmitted by an angel (see Luke 2:10). An ensemble of angels gave a good news concert now sung as "Gloria in Excelsis Deo," glory to God in the highest (see Luke 2:14). Angels were playing a welcome record of *good news*! This is the central message of Christmas, and it forms the heart of the gospel.

Angels We Have Heard on High

Come to Bethlehem and see
Him Whose birth the angels sing;
Come, adore on bended knee,
Christ the Lord, the newborn King

Gloria in excelsis deo
Gloria in excelsis deo.[1]

Dear Father, I live in a critical and cynical world. Teach me to focus on what You are doing that is good and holy, rather than on what is evil and wrong. May those around me know more of what I am for than what I am against. Make me an ambassador of good news. Amen.

Day 20

ZECHARIAH SINGS *a* PRIESTLY SONG

Praise be to the Lord, the God of Israel, because he has come to his people and redeemed them.

Luke 1:68

ZECHARIAH WAS A PRIEST at the time of Jesus' birth. He was an old man when the angel Gabriel disclosed to him that his elderly wife, Elizabeth, was going to have a baby boy. He doubted the message of the heavenly visitor and was penalized for his unbelief and sentenced to silence. After John the Baptist was born, people wanted to name the baby after his father. But Zechariah complied with the angel's directives and wrote out, "His name is John." Once he wrote the name John, Zechariah began to speak again. (See Luke 1:5–22, 57–64.)

Then "Zechariah was filled with the Holy Spirit and prophesied" (verse 67). His hymn is called "The Benedictus," meaning
"Praise Be," after Zechariah's opening words of his song. His rendi-
tion spoke of the redemption of God and His mercy shown to His
people (Luke 1:68, 72, 78). Woven throughout the Benedictus is
the theme that God *remembers His promises.* The priest reminded
his hearers that the Lord honored the words spoken by His holy
prophets "long ago" (Luke 1:70). The Lord had remembered "his
holy covenant" (Luke 1:72). The Lord fulfilled "the oath he swore"
(Luke 1:73) to Abraham.

God's promises are remembered even when—*often* when—it
appears to be too late. The tenth and final plague of Egypt broke
the empire's back, and Israel's four-hundred-year bondage was
finally over. Hundreds of years of silence between the Old and
New Testaments had prompted many to think that the Messiah
would never come; the prophecies would be unfulfilled. But "when
the set time had fully come, God sent his Son, born of a woman,
born under the law, to redeem those under the law, that we might
receive adoption to sonship" (Galatians 4:4–5). The lame man of
John 5 had been handicapped for thirty-eight years prior to his
healing. The blind man of John 9 had been afflicted since birth.

The Lord does not have amnesia. He remembers His promises. Adoniram Judson embraced this *posture of faith* when he trusted in God to fulfill his missionary calling in Burma. "Years went by without a single convert, but he refused to be discouraged. When a member of the Mission Board in America wrote, deploring the lack of results, and inquired concerning the prospects, this intrepid ambassador of Christ replied, 'The prospects are as bright as the promise of God.'"[1] What followed? At his death, the Burmese church had seven thousand members.[2]

O Come, O Come, Emmanuel

O come, O come, Emmanuel,
And ransom captive Israel,
That mourns in lonely exile here,
Until the Son of God appear.
Rejoice! Rejoice! Emmanuel
Shall come to thee, O Israel.[3]

Dear Father, please pardon me for not holding on to Your promises in Scripture. I can be very demanding if the answers to my prayers are delayed. Remind me that delayed is not denied. Give me the gift of perseverance and remind me to look at the scrapbook of my Christian journey and realize Your faithfulness. Amen.

Day 21

KING *of* KINGS!
LORD *of* LORDS!

On coming to the house, they saw the child with his mother Mary, and they bowed down and worshiped him. Then they opened their treasures and presented him with gifts of gold, frankincense and myrrh. And having been warned in a dream not to go back to Herod, they returned to their country by another route.

Matthew 2:11–12

CAN YOU IMAGINE standing before a king and then asking him where you can find and worship the real King? This is the exact scenario that occurred in Matthew 2. The group that ventured the precarious question was the Magi, otherwise known as wise men. The Magi were, among other things, astronomers who observed the constellations and noticed a new star in the eastern sky. They followed this star to the Jerusalem area, where they queried Herod, who was disturbed by the inquiry for the true King. Herod's fear spread to all of Jerusalem (Matthew 2:3), so he summoned Jewish leaders who consulted prophecy and discovered Bethlehem was to be the birthplace of this powerful ruler. During a secret meeting with the Magi, the king commissioned them to go to Bethlehem and then return so that he could also go and worship this new leader.

The Magi departed from Herod and the special star escorted them to a house (see Matthew 2:9–11) where the young child, not a newborn baby, was living. These men were not worshiping the baby Jesus at the manger, despite the nativity displays that place them at that location. Overcome with joy at finding the highly touted little boy, they presented precious gifts: gold, a highly valued mineral commodity; frankincense, a fragrant gum resin; and myrrh, an orange-colored resin used in cosmetics and perfumes, and as a pain-killer and embalming fluid.

We know Herod's plan was not to worship Jesus but to eliminate Him. Would the Magi return and disclose the location of the boy King? No! They were warned in a dream to follow another path home, and Herod was left not knowing where the threat could be extinguished. Per an angel's instructions, Joseph and Mary left that very night and escaped to Egypt. Tragedy followed when Herod realized the visitors from the East did not return to disclose where his competition could be found: "When Herod realized that he had been outwitted by the Magi, he was furious, and he gave orders to kill all the boys in Bethlehem and its vicinity who were two years old and under, in accordance with the time he had learned from the Magi" (Matthew 2:16). Demographers assess that Bethlehem's population of males age two and under would have been around twenty-five in a town of approximately two thousand inhabitants. The "monster of the Christmas story" brought wailing and weeping to a multitude of families because his reign had been threatened and his paranoia had spiked.

King of Kings
Lord of Lords

Though Jesus was not their king, the Magi traveled considerable distance, at considerable expense, and at considerable risk in light of Herod's disposition. Their comfort, their convenience, their resources, and their lives were all spent to worship Jesus. This is powerful modeling by the Magi: because of a heaven-sent dream, they fooled an earthly ruler, and because of a heaven-sent star, they worshiped the King of Kings and Lord of Lords!

Who Is He in Yonder Stall?

Who is He in yonder stall,
At whose feet the shepherds fall?
'Tis the Lord! Oh, wondrous story!
'Tis the Lord, the King of glory!
At His feet we humbly fall.
Crown Him, crown Him, Lord of all.[1]

Dear Lord of heaven and earth, I am inspired and humbled by the example of the Magi who traveled so far, and who gave and risked so much to worship Jesus. This Christmas may the exaltation of Your Son be my first focus, and may He be the primary center of my holiday season. Amen.

Day 22

IS FEASTING *or* FASTING MORE APPROPRIATE?

The shepherds returned, glorifying and praising God for all the things they had heard and seen, which were just as they had been told.

Luke 2:20

IS FEASTING OR FASTING more appropriate in the Advent season? Is Ebenezer Scrooge proper at Christmas gatherings? Should we be more like the Puritans, who downplayed Christmas?

As you survey the first Christmas, you will discover it is marked by *profound celebration*. "My soul glorifies the Lord," was the exclamation of Mary when she discovered she was God's choice to give birth to the Savior of the world (Luke 1:46). John the Baptist leaped in Elizabeth's womb when she encountered Mary of

Nazareth (see Luke 1:41–42). We have seen that the angelic choir broke forth with "Glory to God in the highest" as they informed the shepherds of the incredibly good news (Luke 2:13–14). After seeing the baby Jesus, Luke recorded that "The shepherds returned, glorifying and praising God for all the things they had heard and seen, which were just as they had been told" (Luke 2:20). We've seen the aged Simeon's reaction when he viewed the baby Jesus on the day of His presentation to God: "Simeon took him in his arms and praised God" (Luke 2:28). And the senior widow, Anna, came right behind Simeon and "gave thanks to God and spoke about the child to all who were looking forward to the redemption of Jerusalem" (Luke 2:38).

As you prepare and navigate your Christmas journey this year, make it a practice to wish men and women a "Merry Christmas" because of the good news that prophecies were fulfilled in Jesus Christ when He was born in Bethlehem to rescue a sinful world. Teach your children and your grandchildren why we celebrate Christmas. They must know the holiday is based on the central figure of our faith, Jesus Christ. Give gifts to those in need and demonstrate what Jesus said: "It is more blessed to give than to receive" (Acts 20:35). Engage in many worship activities—the word *Christmas* means "the mass (or worship) of Christ." Read

the Christmas story from Luke 2 prior to opening your gifts. If you have small children at your celebration, you may want to read just Luke 2:1–7; the Scripture reading can grow longer as the children grow older. Have a birthday cake for Jesus!

The birth of Jesus Christ was marked with *celebration, exaltation, joy,* and *jubilation,* so Ebenezer Scrooge should have no place among Mary, the angels, the shepherds, and Simeon and Anna, who modeled enthusiastic gratitude to God for the birth of His Son. Douglas Wilson, in his Christmas book, *God Rest Ye Merry,* asserted, "Our words should sound like good news and our lives should smell like good news."[1]

Joy to the World

Joy to the world, the Lord is come!
Let earth receive her King;
Let every heart prepare Him room,
And heaven and nature sing,
And heaven and nature sing,
And heaven, and heaven, and nature sing.[2]

Dear Father of our Lord Jesus Christ, may my words sound like good news this Christmas season and may my life smell like good news so that I may share with others the joy of the first Christmas that has been transferred to my heart and soul!

ETERNAL LIFE

He has helped his servant Israel, remembering to be merciful to Abraham and his descendants forever, just as he promised our ancestors.

Luke 1:54–55

THE WORDS ABOVE are from the exchange between the angel Gabriel and Mary when he informed her she would bear a son conceived by the Holy Spirit. In the angel's message, he referenced the promises of God made long ago to Abraham that extended to his family and the Jewish people, forever.

In our contemporary celebration of Christmas, we often decorate evergreens. These trees symbolize eternal life for many who display them. This custom of including evergreens in Christmas decor dates back almost one thousand years to when Saint Boniface, who converted the Germanic people to Christianity, came across a group of pagans worshiping an oak tree. Saint Boniface cut down the oak tree, and according to one legend, noticed beyond

the fallen oak a young fir tree, shaped like a church steeple, pointing to heaven. Noting its evergreen foliage, Saint Boniface declared it the tree of the Christ child and that it be brought indoors.[1]

The heavenly ambassador's message to Mary featured grand ideas associated with the birth of her child (see Luke 1:31–33). The angel said His name would be Jesus, which means "the Lord saves," and that the child would be great. The Greek word for "great" is *megas*, from which we derive the English word *mega*. The angel said Mary's son would be given the title "Son of the Most High." And her offspring, born in partnership with the Holy Spirit, would one day sit on David's throne and reign over a Kingdom with no end. Jesus would administrate over an eternal Kingdom—one that had *no expiration date*.

This "evergreen" message would be featured and woven throughout the New Testament. Jesus assigned eternal life to everyone who believed in Him: "I am the resurrection and the life. The one who believes in me will live, even though they die; and whoever lives by believing in me will never die" (John 11:25–26). I recite these verses every time I stand in front of my mother and father's grave sites. Later in John 14:19, Jesus made this eternal claim for His followers: "Because I live, you also will live." And Paul articulated "evergreen" theology in 1 Corinthians 15:22–23, when he connected Christ's resurrection to our own: "For as in Adam all die, so in Christ all will be made alive. But each in turn: Christ, the firstfruits; then, when he comes, those who belong to him."

Green is a very appropriate color integrated into the Christmas color scheme. If it points to the eternal life offered by Jesus and His Kingdom, which never expires, then it speaks to the heart of our planet's visitation by the Son of God, who came to take away the sting of death and provide for us everlasting, unending life!

Joyful, Joyful, We Adore Thee

Joyful, joyful, we adore Thee,
God of glory, Lord of love;
Hearts unfold like flow'rs before Thee,
Op'ning to the sun above.

Melt the clouds of sin and sadness;
Drive the dark of doubt away;
Giver of immortal gladness,
Fill us with the light of day![2]

Heavenly Father, Christmas may be celebrated from year to year, but impress upon my thinking that its message stretches into eternity. Though I am mortal, because of Jesus, I have an immortal shelf life. I may one day succumb to physical death, but that moment will be replaced by life that is eternal.

Day 24

THE COLOR
SILVER

For you know that it was not with perishable things such as silver
or gold that you were redeemed from the empty way of life handed
down to you from your ancestors, but with the precious blood of
Christ, a lamb without blemish or defect.

1 Peter 1:18–19

SILVER IS A PROMINENT COLOR in the decorating
schemes of Christmas. It is probably the third most
popular color in the Christmas palette, behind red
and green.

The word *silver* is used 305 times in the Bible to indicate pros-
perity or to reveal value. Silver is mentioned in Genesis 13:2 to
help indicate Abraham's massive wealth. Silver is compared to the
Word of God in Psalm 12:6: "The words and promises of the LORD
are pure words, like silver refined in an earthen furnace, purified
seven times" (AMP). Proverbs 3:14 escalates the benefits of wisdom

by declaring it "more profitable than silver." Matthew 26:15 details the desirability of silver and casts it as so alluring that Judas, one of Jesus' twelve disciples, agreed to betray Him for thirty pieces of it. Luke 15:8–9 illustrates the worth of one lost soul in the parable of the lost silver coin. Finally, in Revelation 18:11–12, silver is an element in the rich portfolio of ungodly Babylon.

In ancient times, slaves had their freedom purchased by silver and gold. They were redeemed by a perishable commodity. But we, who are slaves to sin, are bought and paid for by the blood of Jesus. Romans 6:6 frames our emancipation with, "So that the body ruled by sin might be done away with, that we should no longer be slaves to sin." This tiny baby in Bethlehem's crude crib was the Lamb of God, who became a substitutionary sacrifice to purchase every sinner who would accept His atoning act of death. Our theme verse above graphically relates this incredible transaction of redemption.

Eventually, Jesus would die to achieve the most valuable gift ever given, what silver or gold could not accomplish: the restoration of man's relationship with God.

Nor Silver nor Gold Hath Obtained My Redemption

Nor silver nor gold hath obtained my redemption;
No riches of earth could have saved my poor soul.
The blood of the cross is my only foundation;
The death of my Savior now maketh me whole.

I am redeemed, but not with silver;
I am bought, but not with gold;
Bought with a price—the blood of Jesus,
Precious price of love untold.[1]

My dearest heavenly Father, I could not purchase my salvation with any precious commodity, even silver or gold. I am indebted to You for spending the body and blood of Jesus as currency to do what I could not do, so that I may be forgiven and free, part of Your family for time and eternity.

Day 25

WISE MEN
SEEK HIM

On coming to the house, they saw the child with his mother Mary,
and they bowed down and worshiped him. Then they opened their
treasures and presented him with gifts of gold, frankincense and
myrrh.

Matthew 2:11

IT IS TAUGHT in American history classes that those who
traveled to America came for one of three reasons: God,
glory, or gold. Gold is the most frequently mentioned metal
in the Bible. It was present in the Garden of Eden (see Genesis 2:8, 12). The Israelites, fearing something had happened to
Moses when he went up to Mount Sinai to receive the Ten Commandments, created a *golden* calf to worship (see Exodus 32:1–4).
The Ark of the Covenant was overlaid with pure gold (see Exodus
25:10–11). And the New Jerusalem is referred to as a city of pure
gold (see Revelation 21:10, 18).

In the New Testament, the value of gold is evident through comparison. In the healing of the crippled beggar, Peter elevated the healing power of Jesus' name above silver or gold (see Acts 3:6–7). Believers who come through suffering possess a genuine faith that is revealed as more precious than gold (see 1 Peter 1:6–7). And our redemption was achieved through the shed blood of Jesus, which is also more precious than gold (see 1 Peter 1:18–19). It is clear that the Scriptures view gold as a standard of mega wealth and value.

We often hear the Christmas hymn "We Three Kings of Orient Are" during the Advent season. Unfortunately, the content is not biblically correct. In the original Greek text of Scripture, the word is *magoi*, wise men, not *basileus*, king. They did present three gifts, but we are not sure of the number of presenters. Some traditions contend there were twelve wise men. Also, these travelers were not from the Orient but from Mesopotamia and Persia, which is modern-day Iran. Another common misconception is evident in the nativity scene, where the wise men are pictured at the manger. As noted in the opening verse, they came to a house.

Despite errors surrounding our understanding of the wise men, we should not miss some key components of their visit. First, they were willing to cover significant distance and invest time and energy so they could worship this "King of the Jews." Second, their gifts were not tokens but precious commodities befitting royalty. Gold, perhaps the most esteemed mineral commodity, was packaged with frankincense, a fragrant resin burned in temple worship, and myrrh, an orange resin used in perfumes. Finally, they did not report back to Herod, obeying God's warning in a dream to go home another way.

Sacrifice, generous stewardship, and obedience to the commands of God are worthy of imitation as we celebrate the birthday of a King.

Wise men seek him

What Child Is This?

So bring Him incense, gold, and myrrh
Come, peasant, king, to own Him
The King of kings salvation brings
Let loving hearts enthrone Him.[1]

Dear giver of every good gift, this Christmas I petition You to enable me to demonstrate sacrifice, generosity, and obedience in my life. Thank You for Your ongoing work in equipping me to live like a wise man.

Day 26

SAINT NICHOLAS: THE ORIGIN *of* SINTERKLAAS

For the wages of sin is death, but the gift of God is eternal life in Christ Jesus our Lord.

Romans 6:23

AS WE COME TO BETHLEHEM in the modern era, there is profound interest in a mythical figure named Santa Claus. The actual forerunner of this bearded Christmas Eve visitor, dressed in red and white, dates to AD 270, in what we now know as Turkey. A man named Nicholas, who lost his wealthy parents to an epidemic when he was a boy, grew up to use his entire inheritance helping the needy. He was known for his benevolence, his love for children, and his concern for sailors and their ships. The Roman emperor Diocletian put him in prison, but he was later released by the emperor

Giver of
Gifts

Constantine, who was friendly to the Christian faith. Saint Nicholas, also known as the bishop of Myra, attended the Christian Council of Nicaea in AD 325, which affirmed the nature of God, the doctrine of the Trinity, and the eternality of Jesus.[1] In many countries gifts are exchanged on December 6, Saint Nicholas Day.

Stories of Saint Nicholas were passed down in European countries. Many traditions developed that found their way to America. The Scandinavians brought the concept of him as an elf. The Dutch brought the name Sinterklaas, which sounds very much like Santa Claus. In 1808, Washington Irving wrote a story about him as a jolly Dutchman. In 1822, Clement Clarke Moore included details from Irving's story when he wrote[2] the poem we now know as "'Twas the Night Before Christmas." He substituted reindeer and a sleigh for Irving's horses and wagons. Later, the cartoonist Thomas Nast gave us a close picture of the Santa Claus we subscribe to today. The evolution of this mythical figure, who travels the world on Christmas Eve, is traced back to a benevolent man in the third century who had the gift of giving and found great joy in dispersing his resources to improve the lives of others. *Christmas is about giving.*

God and His children engage in giving gifts to commemorate the greatest and most priceless gift of all, Jesus. Our Lord Himself made this appraisal recorded in Acts 20:35: "It is more blessed to give than to receive." Jesus modeled and promoted this concept, Saint Nicolas demonstrated this most vividly, and we have the privilege and opportunity to carry forth this principle in our Christmas celebrations in the modern era.

Give of Your Best to the Master

Give of your best to the Master;
Give of the strength of your youth;
Throw your soul's fresh, glowing ardor
Into the battle for truth.
Jesus has set the example,
Dauntless was He, young and brave;
Give Him your loyal devotion;
Give Him the best that you have.[3]

Dear most lavish giver of all, You gave the most precious and priceless gift of all. Keep me from being caught up in receiving gifts unless it is receiving Jesus and the grace He provides. As I journey through the Christmas season, inspire me to realize the blessedness of giving so that others may see "Christ in [me], the hope of glory" (Colossians 1:27).

Day 27

THE ADVENT WREATH: ANTICIPATING HIS COMING

The true light that gives light to everyone was coming into the world.

John 1:9

THE TERM *ADVENT* comes from the Latin word *adventus,* which means "arrival" or "coming." Many churches feature an Advent wreath as a symbolic way of counting down to Christmas Day. The wreath is typically made of evergreen branches that convey the meaning of eternal life. The four outer candles on the wreath are lit one at a time on the four Sundays that precede Christmas. They signify the

ADVENT

waiting that takes place until the fifth candle, the Christ Candle,
is lit on Christmas Eve or Christmas Day.

Each of the four outer candles portrays a particular theme. The
candles vary in color, depending on the tradition the church is following, but often three are purple and one is pink. The sequence
can be as follows: on the first Sunday a purple candle is lit, communicating *hope*; on the second Sunday another purple candle is
lit, communicating *love*; on the third Sunday many churches light
the pink candle, which stands for *joy*, as anticipation of Christmas
is drawing near; on the fourth Sunday, the third purple candle is
lit, with the theme of *peace*. Finally, on December 24 or December
25, the center white candle is lit, which proclaims to the worshipers that *Christ has come—He is born*!

The lighting of the candles heralds a message that the world was
in darkness prior to the coming of Jesus. In fact, Isaiah prophesied
seven hundred years before Jesus' birth with this identical theme:
"The people *walking in darkness have seen a great light*; on those living in the land of deep darkness a light has dawned" (Isaiah 9:2,
emphasis added). Matthew would quote this prophecy when Jesus
began His world-changing ministry in Galilee: "The people living
in darkness have seen a great light; on those living in the land of

the shadow of death a light has dawned" (Matthew 4:16). The Jewish people had experienced four hundred years of prophetic silence prior to the birth of Jesus. No prophecy had been recorded from the time of Malachi to the opening acts of Gabriel's visitation to declare Jesus would be born.

At Christmastime, the Advent celebration bids Christians to experience the anticipation of Christ's long-awaited birth, to celebrate Christ and all that His coming means in the present, and it gives the opportunity to anticipate the fulfillment of Jesus' promise in the future—His coming again!

O Come, All Ye Faithful

Yea, Lord, we greet Thee,
Born this happy morning;
O Jesus, to Thee be all glory given;
Word of the Father, now in flesh appearing.

O come, let us adore Him, O come, let us adore Him,
O come, let us adore Him, Christ the Lord.[1]

Dear Father, Son, and Holy Spirit, I am grateful for the symbols that remind me of Jesus' first coming and prompt me to anticipate His second coming. As the candles are lit in my church during Advent, remind me that You always make true Your promises. Thank You for bringing Jesus' light into the world and into my own life!

Day 28

THE SAVIOR'S SEASON

Suddenly a great company of the heavenly host appeared with the angel, praising God and saying, "Glory to God in the highest heaven, and on earth peace to those on whom his favor rests."

Luke 2:13–14

THE ANGEL CHOIR gave us this short hymn in the verses above in response to a single angel's announcement to the shepherds, "Today in the town of David a *Savior* has been born to you; *he is the Messiah, the Lord*" (verse 11, emphasis added). And so began the first celebration of the birth of Jesus Christ, which we now call *Christmas*.

There would be an ever-expanding symphony of praise. First the angels, then the shepherds, followed by Simeon and Anna. And after the baby had grown into a small child and Mary and Joseph had moved into a house, wise men came from the East. They had made their way from Medo-Persia to inquire where this prophetic

The Only Reason

child, who had a constellation in the sky, could be found. Jesus was the centerpiece of all this human and divine jubilation. Indeed, without Him fulfilling prophecy and wrapping Himself in humanity, there is no reason for Christmas because there is no Christ!

It is incumbent upon us who claim to be believers, disciples, followers, or imitators of Jesus to take stock in whether Jesus is still the *reason for the season*. Do we still value the primary reason for observing Christmas: exalting God the Father for sending His Son and worshiping Jesus for bringing peace to our planet, and indeed to our individual lives? As we do the inventory of our investment portfolio regarding this Christian holiday, we may discover that our shopping for gifts may take precedence over our thanksgiving for *the Gift*.

We may find ourselves spiritually depleted after a post-Thanksgiving calendar that runs straight through December 25 and then into a New Year's celebration just seven days later. If so, it is time to recalibrate the Christmas holiday. It is incumbent upon the people of God to set the Christmas agenda. "If not us, who?" "If not now, when?"

Let's not switch the price tags. The famous quote, attributed to many famous people, is relevant: *Jesus is the reason for the Christmas season!*

The First Noel

The first Noel the angel did say
was to certain poor shepherds in fields as they lay,
in fields where they
lay keeping their sheep,
on a cold winter's night that was so deep.

Noel, Noel, Noel, Noel,
born is the King of Israel.[1]

Dear heavenly Father, there are so many distractions built into the modern observance of this sacred Christmas holiday. Please help me to focus on Your Son and my Savior and Lord, Jesus Christ. My heart's desire is to make Him the centerpiece of my celebration and worship.

MAKE HIM ROOM

Where is the one who has been born king of the Jews? We saw his star when it rose and have come to worship him.

Matthew 2:2

THE WORD CHRISTMAS is derived from *Cristes Maesse*, meaning the "Mass of Christ" or the "Worship of Christ." The Middle English term first appeared in AD 1038. The abbreviated version of Christmas, Xmas, is derived from the fact that the Greek letter X (chi) is the first letter of the Greek word *Christos*, which became *Christ* in English. Christmas was first celebrated on December 25, AD 336, during the reign of Constantine, the Roman emperor.

The priority of worship is evident in the account of the first Christmas in the Gospels: from the angels and the shepherds, to Simeon and Anna, to the Magi from the East.

What has happened to Christmas? It has become a stressful holiday that brings out the worst in many people who observe it. The Holmes-Rahe Stress Inventory allocated a rating of twelve to major holidays, which is almost half the rating given to remodeling a home.[1]

God's people must pray for Him to open opportunities to experience and express this holiday in a holy way. Attending Christian services and inviting family and friends to come along is important. Sharing our gifts and resources with others can be an act of service and worship. I have written stories wrapped around the holiday that have a Christian theme and point the hearers to Christ, the centerpiece of Christmas. Use whatever gift you have to serve others, remembering the words of Jesus, "Whatever you did for one of the least of these brothers and sisters of mine, you did for me" (Matthew 25:40).

Another way to cultivate a Christmas culture of worship is by developing traditions that highlight Christ and the Christian faith. In our family, we always read the Christmas story in Luke 2 before we open our gifts. We sing "Happy Birthday" to Jesus and eat a cake in His honor. Worship can and should be a priority of God's people as we celebrate the coming of Jesus and let people know He is coming again!

MAKE HIM room

Good Christian Men, Rejoice

Good Christian men, rejoice
with heart and soul and voice;
give ye heed to what we say:
Jesus Christ was born today.
Ox and ass before Him bow,
and He is in the manger now.
Christ is born today!
Christ is born today![2]

Dear Father, so many aspects of our modern culture crowd out the mandate and privilege to worship You. Please disperse the distractions and allow me to make the worship of You and Your Son my first priority in life through the Holy Spirit.

Day 30

GOD SENT HIS SON

But when the set time had fully come, God sent his Son, born of a woman, born under the law, to redeem those under the law, that we might receive adoption to sonship.

Galatians 4:4–5

S O MANY PREDICTIONS had been made concerning a Messiah, a Deliverer who would come and free men from bondage. Many leaders envisioned this man as an emancipator who would come as a conquering king and liberate them from the empires that ruled over them. The Assyrians, Babylonians, Persians, Greeks, and, at the time of Jesus' birth, the Romans had established empires that swallowed up the land of Palestine.

Between Malachi and the New Testament era, there had been four hundred years of silence. Not a single prophecy had been recorded. What happened to all the prophetic promises? Did the

God of Abraham, Isaac, and Jacob have amnesia? Would the slavery of the nations that chained Israel go on without abatement? It is honest to say that the hopes of many had evaporated. Generations had come and gone and no divine personality had appeared to satisfy the cries and yearnings of a subjugated people. Hindsight enables us to see that the more important bondage was spiritual and so was the Kingdom to be established. But as the apostle Paul wrote in Galatians, certain conditions had to be in place, certain criteria had to be met, certain circumstances had to be in play, and then it would be the *fullness of time*.

Into that fullness, into time and space, stepped Jesus, to validate the prophets like Isaiah, Jeremiah, and Micah, who had, by faith, declared that a Redeemer, a Savior, would come to earth.

History makes us aware that Jesus' birth was timely because the Romans allowed the spread of different religions, transportation allowed for the dissemination of information, and the Greek language, because of Alexander the Great and his conquests, was recognized and spoken around the globe. Because the New Testament is written in Greek, it could be understood around the known world.

When history was ripe and ready, God sent His Son, and salvation was placed in the womb of a virgin. His birth would herald a new age of miracles and messages to demonstrate the love and power of God through Jesus Christ. Paul put it in these definitive terms: "For no matter how many promises God has made, they are 'Yes' in Christ" (2 Corinthians 1:20).

Jesus is the *fulfiller of the fullness of time* and the *fulfiller of all the promises pledged by God the Father*!

Hail to the Lord's Anointed

Hail to the Lord's Anointed,
great David's greater Son!
Hail in the time appointed,
His reign on earth begun!
He comes to break oppression,
to set the captive free;
to take away transgression,
and rule in equity.[1]

Dear Lord, so often my faith is short-lived. Enable me to grow in my trust of Your Word so that I may never give up on Your promises. May my heart be firm, my mind resolute, because You are faithful and true to what You say You will do.

Day 31

COME
to the PARTY

For in him all things were created: things in heaven and on earth, visible and invisible, whether thrones or powers or rulers or authorities; all things have been created through him and for him.

Colossians 1:16

JOSEPH SIMPSON COOK wrote a beautiful Christmas carol in 1919 that starts,

Gentle Mary laid her Child
Lowly in a manger;
There He lay, the undefiled,
To the world a stranger.[1]

Perhaps in a cognitive sense, the world did not expect or recognize the Christ child. In many ways Jesus' coming would have been undetected except for the angels informing the shepherds that a Savior had been born in Bethlehem. Often in Christian preaching and teaching, He is described as a guest or a stranger who is treated as an outsider.

But it should be mentioned that in many ways Jesus was the host not the guest. Every aspect of the Christmas story—the animals, the manger, the earth and skies that formed a platform for His bed and canopied over His birthplace—was made by Him. He authored the story from beginning to end, not only creating all elements of it but also starring in it. Although viewed as a stranger, He choreographed the prophecies of old and supervised the details of the virgin birth of the Messiah Himself.

Christmas is hosted by heaven, and every aspect of the greatest story ever told was written, ordered, and fulfilled by Jesus. This special holiday we observe year after year had its roots in a holy God and in His Son, who designed a plan to deal with mankind's

inability to stay away from temptation and escape the cancer of sin. A. W. Tozer wrote in *Christ the Eternal Son,*

> This was the eternal One. He had come into His own world. While we often talk about Him being our guest here, it is not Jesus Christ who is the guest. We talk about making God partner in our affairs, but I dare to tell people that they should stop patronizing Jesus Christ. He is not the guest here—He is the host.[2]

And all who have accepted His gracious offer of forgiveness and new life are grateful for His invitation to His party!

Come, Thou Long Expected Jesus

Come, Thou long expected Jesus,
born to set Thy people free;
from our fears and sins release us,
let us find our rest in Thee.
Israel's strength and consolation,
hope of all the earth thou art;
dear desire of every nation,
joy of every longing heart.

Born Thy people to deliver,
born a child and yet a King,
born to reign in us forever,
now Thy gracious kingdom bring.
By Thine own eternal spirit
rule in all our hearts alone;
by Thine all sufficient merit,
raise us to Thy glorious throne.[3]

Dear Lord Jesus, remind me that Your coming into our world was not a coincidence; it was Your creation from start to finish. I am so thankful You wrote me into Your story of grace and love.

Day 32

A FOREVER KING

He will reign over Jacob's descendants forever; his Kingdom will never end.

Luke 1:33

EVEN SECULAR MAN LONGS to live forever. The pyramids of Egypt were built to last an eternity. In modern times, the musical *Fame* featured a song by the same title that started with the singer claiming she was going to live forever. The angel Gabriel addressed this longing for eternal life in his address to Mary, a teenager in Nazareth. His message to her in Luke 1:32 was filled with superlatives when he guaranteed that she would bear the Son of the Most High, that her Son would be great (*mega*) and would one day receive the throne of His father David (the greatest king of Israel). Then Gabriel revealed that this child would have a *forever* reign and His Kingdom would never *end*. The word for *forever* in the Greek means eternal or everlasting, it speaks of infinite elasticity. The word *end* is even more interesting. The Greek word is *telos*, meaning "the limit at

His
Kingdom
will
never
end

which a person or thing ceases to be what he or it was up to that point."[1] The divine messenger literally stated there will never be a *telos*, an end, to this Kingdom!

Throughout His life, Jesus was the visible picture of the invisible God. His promises to His followers, those who receive the salvation He offers, have forever overtones. At the raising of His friend Lazarus from the dead, Jesus made this incredible proclamation: "I am the resurrection and the life. The one who believes in me will live, even though they die; and whoever lives by believing in me will never die" (John 11:25–26). He connects our destiny with His own in John 14:19: "Because I live, you also will live." And Paul aligns with this theology in 1 Corinthians 15:22–23: "For as in Adam all die, so in Christ all will be made alive. But each in turn: Christ, the firstfruits; then, when he comes, *those who belong to him*" (emphasis added).

Jesus has grafted us into His Kingdom, which *has no expiration date*. This truth is a part of the Christmas message we must share to a world searching for an extension to mortality.

Jesus, Son of God Most High

Jesus, Son of God most high,
God from all eternity,
Born as man to live and die,
Hear us, holy Jesus.

Leaving Thine eternal throne,
Making mortal cares Thine own,
Making God's compassion known,
Hear us, holy Jesus.

By Thy life, so lone and still,
By Thy waiting to fulfill
In its time Thy Father's will,
Hear us, holy Jesus.

May we mark the pattern fair
Of Thy life of work and prayer,
And for truth all perils dare,
Hear us, holy Jesus.

Bid us come, at last, to Thee,
And forever perfect be,
Where Thy glory we shall see,
Hear us, holy Jesus.[2]

Dear Father, thank You for providing a way through Jesus to escape the penalty of our sins and to be ushered into salvation, which carries the promise of forever life!

NOTES

Day 2 God Became a Single Cell

1. C. S. Lewis, *Mere Christianity* (San Francisco: Harper Collins, 1952), 178. *Mere Christianity* by CS Lewis © copyright 1942, 1943, 1944, 1952 CS Lewis Pte Ltd. Extract used with permission.
2. Josiah Gilbert Holland, "There's a Song in the Air," 1875, public domain.

Day 3 Serendipity

1. C. S. Lewis, *The Last Battle* (New York: Harper Collins, 1984), 177. *The Last Battle* by CS Lewis © copyright 1956 CS Lewis Pte Ltd. Extract used with permission.
2. Nahum Tate, "While Shepherds Watched Their Flocks by Night," 1700, public domain.

Day 4 The Cradle That Rocked the World

1. Mary Elizabeth Coleridge, "I Saw a Stable," 1897, public domain.
2. Henry Barraclough, "Ivory Palaces," 1915, public domain.

Day 5 A Star to Guide

1. William Chatterton Dix, "As with Gladness, Men of Old," 1859, public domain.

Day 6 Extraordinary!

1. Anonymous, "God Rest Ye Merry, Gentlemen," eighteenth century, public domain.

Day 7 The Word Becomes Flesh

1. Henry Ramsden Bramley and John Stainer, "The Incarnation," 1871, public domain.

Day 8 Prophecy Fulfilled

1. John Mason Neale, trans., "Of the Father's Love Begotten," 1851, public domain.

Day 9 The Ironies of Christmas

1. *Merriam-Webster's Collegiate Dictionary*, 11th ed. (2020), s.v. "irony," www.merriam-webster.com/dictionary/irony.
2. Josiah Gilbert Holland, "There's a Song in the Air," 1875, public domain.

Day 10 The Politics of Christmas

1. James Montgomery, "Angels from the Realms of Glory," 1816, public domain.

Day 11 Marvelous Mystery

1. Chalcedonian Creed, Council of Chalcedon, 451, accessed December 14, 2023, https://www.orthodoxpath.org/catechisms-and-articles/council-of-chalcedon-451ad.
2. John Morison, "The People That in Darkness Sat," 1781, public domain.

Day 12 Bread of Life

1. Lucy Neeley Adams, "O Little Town of Bethlehem—Lyrics and Story behind Popular Christmas Carol," Crosswalk.com, January 15, 2019, https://www.crosswalk.com/special-coverage/christmas-and-advent/o-little-town-of-bethlehem-1457973.html.
2. Quoted in John Lloyd and John Mitchinson, *If Ignorance Is Bliss, Why Aren't There More Happy People? Smart Quotes for Dumb Times* (New York: Harmony, 2008), 313.
3. Phillips Brooks, "O Little Town of Bethlehem," 1868, public domain.

Day 13 Peace on Earth

1. Justin Taylor, "The True Story Behind 'I Heard the Bells on Christmas Day," The Gospel Coalition, December 21, 2014, www.thegospelcoalition.org/blogs/justin-taylor/the-story-of-pain-and-hope-behind-i-heard-the-bells-on-christmas-day.
2. Don Richardson, *Peace Child* (Ventura, CA: Regal, 2005), 164–183.
3. Henry Wadsworth Longfellow, "I Heard the Bells on Christmas Day," 1864, public domain.

Day 14 Holy Night

1. Robert K. Brown and Mark R. Norton, eds., *The One Year Book of Hymns* (Wheaton, IL: Tyndale House, 1995), December 24.
2. Joseph Mohr, "Silent Night, Holy Night," 1816, public domain.

Day 15 Angels Sing

1. W. E. Vine, Merrill Unger, William White, Jr., *Vine's Complete Expository Dictionary of Old and New Testament Words* (Grand Rapids: Thomas Nelson, 1996), 26.
2. Charles Wesley, "Hark, the Herald Angels Sing," 1739, public domain.

Day 16 Promises Kept

1. Quoted by Laura Newberry, "The pandemic has amplified ageism. 'It's open season for discrimination' against older adults," *Los Angeles Times*, May 1, 2020, https://www.latimes.com/california/story/2020-05-01/coronavirus-pandemic-has-amplified-ageism.
2. William Chatterton Dix, "What Child Is This?," 1865, public domain.

Day 17 What Manner of Love

1. Dorothy L. Sayers, *The Greatest Drama Ever Staged* (London: Hodder & Stoughton, 1938).
2. Christina Georgina Rossetti, "Love Came Down at Christmas" (poem also published under the title "Christmastide"), 1885, public domain.

Day 18 Joy in the Forecast

1. Joseph Simpson Cook, "Gentle Mary Laid Her Child," 1919, public domain.

Day 19 The Flash of Christmas: Good News!

1. French Carol translated by James Chadwick, "Angels We Have Heard on High," 1862, public domain.

Day 20 Zechariah Sings a Priestly Song

1. Eugene Myers Harrison, "Adoniram Judson: Apostle of the Love of Christ in Burma," in *Giants of the Missionary Trail* (Chicago: Scripture Press, 1954), reprinted at Wholesome Words, accessed July 18, 2023, https://www.wholesomewords.org/missions/giants/biojudson2.html.
2. A. Scott Moreau (ed.) *Evangelical Dictionary of World Missions* (Grand Rapids: Baker Books, 2000), 529.
3. John Mason Neale, translator, "O Come, O Come, Emmanuel," 1851, public domain.

Day 21 King of Kings! Lord of Lords!

1. B. R. Hanby, "Who Is He in Yonder Stall?," 1866, public domain.

Day 22 Is Feasting or Fasting More Appropriate?

1. Douglas Wilson, *We Wish Ye Merry: Why Christmas Is the Foundation for Everything* (Moscow, ID: Canon Press, 2012), 88.
2. Isaac Watts, "Joy to the World," 1719, public domain.

Day 23 Eternal Life

1. Zteve T Evans, "The Legend of Saint Boniface and the Thunder Oak and the Origin of the Christmas Tree," Under the Influence!, December 12, 2022, https://ztevetevans.wordpress.com/2022/12/12/the-legend-of-saint-boniface-and-the-thunder-oak-and-the-origin-of-the-christmas-tree.

2. Henry J. van Dyke, "Joyful, Joyful, We Adore Thee," 1907, public domain.

Day 24 The Color Silver

1. James Martin Gray, "Nor Silver nor Gold Hath Obtained My Redemption," 1908, public domain.

Day 25 Wise Men Seek Him

1. William Chatterton Dix, "What Child Is This?" (poem originally published under the title "The Manger Throne"), 1865, public domain.

Day 26 Saint Nicholas: The Origin of Sinterklaas

1. "Who Is St. Nicholas?," St. Nicholas Center, accessed December 14, 2023, https://www.stnicholascenter.org/who-is-st-nicholas.

2. Some believe the poem to be written by Henry Livingston Jr.

3. Howard B. Grose, "Give of Your Best to the Master," 1902, public domain.

Day 27 The Advent Wreath: Anticipating His Coming

1. John Francis Wade, "O Come, All Ye Faithful," 1744, public domain.

Day 28 The Savior's Season

1. Anonymous, "The First Noel," 1833, public domain.

Day 29 Make Him Room

1. "The Homes-Rahe Stress Inventory," The American Institute of Stress, accessed December 14, 2023, https://www.stress.org/wp-content/uploads/2019/04/stress-inventory-1.pdf.

2. John Mason Neale, trans., "Good Christian Men, Rejoice," 1853, public domain.

Day 30 God Sent His Son

1. James Montgomery, "Hail to the Lord's Anointed," 1821, public domain.

Day 31 Come to the Party

1. Joseph Simpson Cook, "Gentle Mary Laid Her Child," 1919, public domain.

2. A. W. Tozer, *Christ the Eternal Son* (Camp Hill, PA: Wingspread, 2009), 63.

3. Charles Wesley, "Come, Thou Long Expected Jesus," 1744, public domain.

Day 32 A Forever King

1. W. E. Vine, Merrill Unger, William White, Jr., *Vine's Complete Expository Dictionary of Old and New Testament Words* (Nashville: Thomas Nelson, 1996), 198.

2. Thomas Benson Pollock, "Jesus, Son of God Most High," 1871, public domain.

Arnold R. Fleagle became a follower of Jesus Christ on April 1 when he was twelve, and he affirms, like Paul, "I became a fool for Christ's sake." He has published poetry, written articles for church magazines, and coauthored or authored fourteen books, including *The Commands of Messiah*. In his teen years he won several writing awards, including a district youth writing contest (where he was the only entry), first place in a newspaper contest, and second place at the Pennsylvania Rotary Leader's Camp. His sermon "The Three Visions of Isaiah" tied for first place in his denomination's message competition.

His purpose in writing is to give clarity to the meaning and power of God's Word. He desires to encourage individuals to accept Jesus Christ as Lord and Savior, and for those already saved, to motivate them to follow Him with courage and obedience.

Arnie has a bachelor of science in education from Shippensburg University, a master of arts in biblical literature from Asbury Theological Seminary, and a doctor of ministry from Gordon-Conwell Theological Seminary. He has served as a senior pastor in five churches and as director of development in the Central District of the Christian and Missionary Alliance. He now serves as an interim pastor for that same district in Ohio.

His marriage to his wife, Faye, has eclipsed fifty years, and they have two sons, Matthew and Marc. They also have the privilege of being Mimi and Pappy to four exceptional grandchildren.

Arnie follows sports at all levels and is a Penn State and Pittsburgh Steelers fan. He collects a number of items, including Christmas nutcrackers, banks, clocks, and milk bottles. His favorite vacation spot is Myrtle Beach.